# watchful

# Previous Works

AFTER ESTRANGEMENT
Peregrine Smith Books 1992

DARK SUMMER
Miami University Press 1999

ARIADNE'S ISLAND
Miami University Press 2002

UNDER THE QUICK
Parlor Press 2009

BLING & FRINGE (Co-authored with Gail Wronsky)
What Books 2009

# watchful   molly bendall

OMNIDAWN PUBLISHING
OAKLAND, CALIFORNIA
2016

Cover photo: "Zebra" by Scotch Macaskill

Cover and interior typefaces: Adobe Garamond Pro and Birch Std

Cover and interior design by Cassandra Smith

Offset printed in the United States
by Edwards Brothers Malloy, Ann Arbor, Michigan
On 55# Glatfelter B18 Antique
Acid Free Archival Quality Recycled Paper

Library of Congress Cataloging-in-Publication Data

Names: Bendall, Molly, author.
Title: Watchful / Molly Bendall.
Description: Oakland, California : Omnidawn Publishing, 2016.
Identifiers: LCCN 2016015125 | ISBN 9781632430212 (softcover : acid-free paper)
Classification: LCC PS3552.E5384 A6 2016 | DDC 811/.54--dc23
LC record available at https://lccn.loc.gov/2016015125

Published by Omnidawn Publishing, Oakland, California
www.omnidawn.com    (510) 237-5472    (800) 792-4957
10  9  8  7  6  5  4  3  2  1
ISBN: 978-1-63243-021-2

*For Vivienne*

In no way had I entered that world; on the contrary, it was rather as if its strangeness had declared itself anew, as if I had actually been allowed for an instant to see something from which as a human being I shall be forever excluded.

Jean-Christophe Bailly
*The Animal Side*

# I

## TRESPASS

## ANIMALS AND SOVEREIGNS

Tricked with trick snow
and a makeshift gate.

Then overstuffed edges terraced and terraced, cool and redundant.

Song sent out light
behind the hills
though not yours or mine,

not near a crestfall or a gorge.
If there had been a landbridge, that might
explain the deep fur.

They're myth because
we slept so long. What lulls us besides the North Star?

Now comes the broadcast

and reassurance. Lean back into everydayness
while some just swan by with the last

of their hardened expression.

A few, a frozen few, have permission,
and the narrow moat

gets my attention. Only when afternoon flashes on it, turns it
doubtful, do they sever the rustling perimeters.

Roamers in spite of the trembling. A bit of weed and wash can make
them elegant.
It's like that in a blink,

and threads take hold. The weather ahead socked in
and stilled
to a gray kittenish shape.

Just for a while
attend
to the rock-quiet.

Murder has taken a sabbatical.
They lumber and harp for new ground in their spherical world.

## A Keen Sense

Not a bothered body or a sleepcoil. He's dislodged

the pretend of it,
and this station's double-crossed
with a new cake, a metal ball.

Only that one really *knows* Kathmandu. The sun treats the soft strands on its back.

So we daze him
or jewel him
with weight when new eyelashes appear

for the stroking. Sham a little for scraps.

Maybe he's in
on racketeering charges.

The knot in my jaw is named
for the one who bolted out.
And a moon-sliver stays in a section of sky. Curtains for him.

Trophies ghost the savanna,

as a clutch of eggs arrives in a forest closet.

Calves, take me walking, we'll recite
with our baskets out.
Have I outstayed the shine beyond yours, rushed in for more sympathetic
looks?

If torments were dresses barkers would twirl. And what's prohibitive—touching
a dewclaw for luck?

This one's a good soldier,
and the condor's wingspan fills the maze.

## BELATEDNESS

Furrows drift and pearl in the sand, does anyone
                                   leave for the hinterlands? A leader

   heads home, woolly and in need of rest
trailing the warp and weft behind him.

                    A circle is the green way to the ground so I read into it,
        read further, and the spiraling horns shoot up and backwards,

they rule the ginko grove, their amplitude is sheer.

   Some pace with their bounty, scratch a bother on a hind leg
                                         then stomp downstairs.

I come here to teach my ear to adore,
                    shape myself as orphan. Call this one the new fashion with
a coxcomb and florid fever. He's ruling in his jagged stole, his gold eyes
fathom the tub

placed on the grass. I halted so suddenly
                    pins fell and my breath backed up. He sings in two vowels,

corrals with some shrill orders. I ask every sky I meet about the age we're in.

   Anyone, anyone leaving with their ledger full?
                    Look inside between this shelter and the antechamber
      and resume
      the tundra laws. This devotion may be an acceptable risk. Then some

      go missing, some go in a flurry,
                    their horns arcing above their heads to another zenith.

## TRESPASS

A glance into the gray, stuttering and flushed.
It's most like treachery except scales
come shedding. I'll wear the fatal expression of being somewhere else.
Tumbled in a dizzy
habitat, scattershot and rigged with watchers.
And young crawl blindly—fuzz striping, nubs for horns.
Their eyes, evening clocks, and a milky way. Still stunned
at the clouds bearing down.

Understand the lure. Thrumming
with green current, love's sort of in a thrall.
I woke to this civic arrangement, peered
down the tunnel.
Heavy in their entourage, they secure a chilly saga,
always for each other, while
I daughter myself, I girl the most
delicate ones, creep up to them nearer the forelocks and swarming flies.

## Season of Perpetrators

They sleep as if their plights were real, they flinch and scrape.

If speed ever once
shivered for them, if a heat thermal came pushing up,

they'd devour their own future and sell off
their fortune: one yard, one boulder.

A green gel comes between us
then springs back so the lens fades to gray, but it's not like floating,
it's closer,
and there's a flap of skin. The keeper

says they're nursing that wound.

Not a scent of threat, more like preening, more like a wedding,
coral trees assemble behind.

Flexing into thought, I'm woozy
with lateness.

Their pompadours are a tangle of magic straw.
I give way
to wide words cast on the hillside, as their pink tongues

stab the black air, rank and sinew steadfast.

## Schooled in Wandering

       Don't watch them with names,
       don't let them drag their tails.

Hardly a face,
it's like a heavy
brow or a cap

wedged down. Slowing up the stare
and my heart, maybe, has a habit.
I blow my hair away,

and they're gaping
and unlocked
like the drone of highways.

She's nuzzling her mate. The swamp's
gotten greedy. If it's summer
with its haws, then we're

in the lawn chairs at midnight.
When I feel a storm stiffen, leaves begin
to steep,

branches fall across
the foot-bridge. That one
swims heavy.

       Don't mercy with their water hideaway.
       Don't stay when its nostrils are tipped up,

boat out until
you don't belong. There's gnawing

under the weather

and hours in the milling.
       I wasn't backing up,
       wasn't calling the chaperone to help hush.

So I'd argue
for a sprawl
close to thunder and the rippling outward.

A bucket's worth and
what's left, something gnarly?
Upside down, a dirty hoof.

# Far Shine in the Park's Pond

King of the pack, you're as mute
as a twinkle. Still, words
match the mumble of winter.
By the time you sing
a table clears, tall grass
bends a path, petals chant
an omen. So
it's merely conjecture,
your suddenness, your
flapping, and hardly worth
considering, even if we count
backwards until ardent green appears.

\*

For this occasion I collected
gold filaments, but don't
remember my first bike.
I shouldn't cling to the empty
spaces as the old logic
does, nor should I stroke
the mossy borders
of the park.
I will admire you this
one last forlorn and silken
time, the blinks that surround
you, portals to shyness.
Whispering won't summon
the hermitage you looked for.

\*

You can't float without
a shudder, maybe
try more locution—
feathers loose, an ideogram.
Why not quiver by car
like any bird would?
Here's your bell, here's
your dusty bolero.
Some like your plot in
slow stitches, some nudge
to let in the calendar.

*

By law I make up shadows
on white, then slide netting
over my face, as
gnats swarm in a dizzy queue.
Barely rustling
you trick the lookers and forfeit
the clouds that pearl
and shift their bundles.
Oh just to see you alone here.
Beholden to doll hair,
I shush all the early risers.
And the wick skims
the liturgy it loves.

## BRAVE THE PATH

Her forest look numbs me when I wake long enough
to feel a tug and soft panting. Only something leopard would rival

      the chill. If circling birds would find the tween, I'd read letters
backwards. Certain, then, my tries would scatter into shining bits

of woe. Antlers lilt
      and fall from the valley. Just a flick of a tail and I'd follow her,
  forfeit my den. Can't catch the deep brown, can't hear the trance
she hears,

and I'd lure her from gate to bow
from shoulder to stern. Would it be better to hold still

and sit by the picnic blaze? Better to wear the maps like skin and fur?
  Because I carry on *here* from where
      I want to be gone.

She's onto me and my foxing moves. Her step
      is a sleeping neighbor, a tremulous relative. Only she
could crush the edges of a spring temple.

I should saddle up now, coax along my dogs of winter,
and launch into the fray. In her domain she's not the vendetta,

      though she might be what lit those sharp claws.

## GROOMING AND PURSUIT


Flocks careen
the warehouses, wings dodge the prickly pear. Pull your mouth strings

and hazard a guess. See what starts
to change, what's on
a hook.

The last line is for Destination Impossible. Like a clever silk net?

A catchall phrase
for taking cover. We'll wake long enough into the lunar spring. I'll try
to detect

your black rosettes
as you bat a frilly wasp from the air.

I'll mend your ear
when we get there, I'll stroke
the deeplasting of your coat. You're

the most elusive, most inclined to puncture a skull. For you find virtue

in a thrall of flapping, for you temper the frantic.
Leave your slab of meat in the sun.

Camouflaged faces lurking
in tangles,

and marauders
trade lupine and hatchweed
for contraband.

Whiskery broom and sage stay low in the grumbling.

When you pretend to be shadow, when you rub
your shoulder on trees,

we measure metal left in stars. Shrapnel glints under my skin.

The others all tomb together
and rise close to the filament. Stealth becomes us, it's what leads us to summer
in this bare place.

## Animal Radiance

The pale rocks and dust: their jurisdiction and their snowblooms.
One mottled shape's

a fleur-de-lys. Forger of sleep,
tracking your mood.

Easy to make a diorama when you're steering

the sky. Their splendid interiority I adopt myself, and I paid for the attraction.

Here's a marvel—
one courts
the other, brings her flesh and decorative leaves.

A blurry noise
weighed through

the trees. Still, I'm sure, craving their suddenness.
A shadow on the fence,

a constellation in my cup, piped in music.

I unstuck the lapsed expressions, find an antler's been shed. No matter
how many times—they must often forget their training.

Cool off
in the shallow lake. Almost on guard, ready to hurry. The side-yard provides

a fastening. He pushes his barrel,
smashes his fruit,

and comes to hide
in brambles.
Fur can glare, even hurt.

# II

## GRASSLAND BUREAUCRACY

# GRASSLAND BUREAUCRACY

More rain and cockles
To bear until I'm
Sure wind is the way
To higher learning
And I'll count
Our breaths, muster
A scare tactic and you might
Vanish like a suspect
Your huge girth in
Transit then into the snags
I like being stretched
To a half-acre and haven't
Panicked yet, I gather
My bag of notions
Tote it along these grounds
I should stride
With more
Force, as your tracks
Mess up
The path and then you go
Piss on your brother
With the twisted
Horns and I'll
Be your witness
Deck yourself out, be like
Hercules, glide
Over harried ground
Cover in your
Pewter pelt feeling the snaps

Through the dark
On a weedy slope
We'd come to a draw,
Give a pass
With your tail, grunt
A divide in the earth
I can't leave
The shimmering for the dim—
See how you stand
Sudden in sizzling heat,
How you fasten on
Tight when the camera
Comes, you're the wiser
For it, caught in bramble,
My foot's a wingbeat,
My hair, an expanse
With old bite marks
Try avoiding my looks, give up
Your *darling* status
I could've come
Down from the canyons
Bringing rancor
I'm so hawk
Now and staying
Just outside the bundle
Of dank rooms
When clutter seeps
Into the dark land

Dare me to move
Down and we'll go
Head first to find
The hammering still persists
Sixteen days and there's
Nothing more to fling
Into the maw
Into your wilderness
How to aim
The spittle, how to
Make it fit
Through winter's motor
I'm as good as fainting
And learned it
From you, having seen
Your graceless aim
And a gun as big
As all get-out
Show me the ambush
The gap in the stairs
It's pay back
Time with a barbed
Wire frame
Alight on it
Perch between
Losing and lurking
Up on the dim
Side of your habitat
I fished for the right
Way around

Learning how
To lead
With hunting pauses
Anything could
Be bought—a new planet
In retrograde
It need not be
A dream, anyone
Can riddle you
The lull starts
In a gallop
Under the sunlight's whistle
I tease you
But I know it's all your
Sorrow, air so crisp
You could sniff
Out the sea and
Be the last
Face in the woods
And charge across any
Terrain you want
But be here on time
In your satiny face
I'm the culprit

Lead me
To the next retreat
I'll set up shop
Near the electrified branches
Pad down the small
Humiliations
Your deep brown gloss,
Thicker than drums
I'm near-ready to own
The dander
You air out
This could be a new place
To be a maverick
Then I'll be
Your dark thought
Pushed to a zigzag
Quiver, soft head to
Soft head
Satellites orbit too close
You cock your head
Their way
Slowness is the mode
Like the weather
I tried to fever it
Closer but I have
No guts and nothing
Was clean about it

Heavy machinery
Shuts off for the day
You find yourself crooked
In your resting place
Why linger
In the world like that?
You'll be deposed
Soon under cotton skies
More quiet more hiding
And I had a haunting
Gaze and a showy
Collarbone once
How do we look now
In the roped-off area?
You need
A comb-through
In the wild
Hundreds of us
Were bounding over
Sand dunes, beyond air
Beyond
Any wreckage we know

# III

# THE QUEUE IN MOTION

## SPECTACLE

His rumble, the way he tears

at the carrion, then leaves a hive for listening.
Tusks bang and glimmer in the sunlight. Can't stoop to interpretation.

I press my mascaraed face
to the fence and see my relation—

he's mangy, has his pounds.
There's an eon that beckons me back, and recognizing the swipe

turning into blazing reason, I tell myself

let the sobbing
take on a rhapsody, let this
strobing outlast my afternoon mind.

The big chrysanthemum flirt with death inside.

A flash down the access road,
playing the system, his cunning restores my empty party.

Every day he's my dream stand-in.

Someone's taught him
when the clock is lit,
the budget's been gored with the low-down.

A gust draws a furrow

in his hair, and stringy meat gets licked away.

Twilight's pulse thrumming like so—
bellowing near my own throat.

## The Queue in Motion

Somehow I knew they'd suffer for me in their spread-out coats
    and rough napes, and I'd steer through their dens,

or punked in lynx, I'd weather the roaming

        highways. And where are you in the shepherd quiet?

Is that you or a decoy of you? Row off to the cooler patches,
go to the corner pagoda
      for ibex tranquility. All I think

of is the wrong route to the trestle I took once, the rumbling train,
      the water's edge
and the loose
kite. A tail for a scarf, a full stop, and at the penny's end,

how some nuzzle the tenterhooks,
      how they teem in damaging weather. They circle until
the grasses lie down. A few sentences rustle,

  the day's unconsoled. I've dreamt up the riddles and figure
      that's where the future is, where the carousel

fleeces in the bright light. Those rearing up, panting in stitches.
an eon spanning the screen, and there's a zeal

      in their hides, and I take to it, reminding me
there's no end to the undergrowth
  and steel shards in the winter clouds.

# SPLENDOR

Be done but be the same. Tuck yourself in, until you're listing
into the fallen zone (It's not so green), and blindfold me
but never take me away. What was
                    wretched and what was fair stays, and I'm afraid

I pawed it, then watched the horrible pulse. And lulled into pitying, into

                    a sleepdrenched day. My kibbitz monger, my squat moon,
my tidal suitcase. Your gigantic wagon

with its warped wheels can't stay home.

                    And bereft without the bared teeth. There's still a self
    like your self on a dusty hill around the world. Leaves evaporate kindly
and don't trouble our alphabet game.

                    Aware of it, aware of the flax, broom, and bluebells,
the offshore breeze. Frost is new and rare, and
    bougainvillea sidles up to the others. Then soon I'll have a nervous system
accounting for it,

but don't buzz or keen. I think our tea time

                                        went west. Your heft promises
all girth, and skin, all surface. What's left? Must have been
bulldozed into a cradle. My skipper stout,
                    my tank magnitude, my gray throb harp-case.

    You've gone peddling. Put a cheek to the cement, I'll take my betters
and shape them like that.

# Monday Guardian

When you're
in too close
the mouse bones soften and settle in tight.

Come down when the tension wires undo. I'd
smoothe a network then,
but you're part missing even as you kick up and up.

Every minute thinks
of passing sky, every milky bowl shuns a sooty back.

I've zeroed
in on your sumptuous reach. Lost when I remember

you most, and then you fall

asleep in the U petals.

I'll be one of those who talks back,
not dainty
too much.
A stone's throw and a sob back to you,

and I'll be one who gnaws at the capillaries

so sing your invitation now,
invite me to inspect

your starter home, place your likeness on the thin green rim.

## CONVERGE IN RAUCOUS BRANCHES

I take to
her shoe-sized hovel and decaying forsythia.
Let's go for the instant snow fall,

get marooned on the stone porch.
Now too, tranquilized,

she'll pad down the gnarled rope, tap the corners in.

Go again. Again. Lift her up
by the scruff.

Pocket the thistle and vole fur,

and this one sings loose and regretful, a pollen-tinted face.
Right as doing. Wait for the drop date.

I'm near emptied
so follow the burned-out drawer

and the plastic shards in
a chain of wind.
Pull a name into the chatter and wed it to
your fixes.

She's got brooding duties and weaves with horsehair and cools
with her shadows.

## Yesterday Orbit

When they're done storming they hide in the little night box.

In a minute knot and knot and poke through
the net. Not a vessel to ride in.

Not a message to misconstrue.
Only wolfish guarding and a long chute to the dark.

Flutter near the gut engine,

bury deep in petal verve.

I don't follow
form
or falling. I hear a click-wish and
want to bask under these canopies.

Warbling's gone sober.
Felted with moss.

Watch,
they'll have scrappy beards when they come
and they'll clock around the bushes.

Vocalists of the snapshot, let me whirl in some string.

## Synchrony

But these are earthbound. Their rules stack up when
vines cover the entryway. I'm too crowded. Hundreds of helmets flock
over the hill's face,

robber barons lurk above the valley. They sniff out the equinox,

and when someone takes a picture it nods and blurs its head,
a shape-shifter now.

Don't you covet their parliament? So final, so shrill in the teeth. To track

their sunken looks, I mistake their silhouettes
for carcasses. I could crown this one with a bruised hat. A twitch in its snout,
grizzly even in its lips.

Who's streaming down
from their roosts in a sudden flush of platinum? I can hear it
in their bumpy dialect, their wanting gazes. My voice blends,

and I match my head to their eyes. If I could rescue

their messages, as willows close in with a ruse of green, I'd
pull my quivering cap on so it's all twice as real.

# IV

# THE SIXTH WAVE

# THE SIXTH WAVE

An enclosure, that's fit
And who's on watch?
   They might piece
The cloud cover
A little warped
   Unfathom a whole
Lot of investors
   Turn every corner
To the last white
Rhinos every one
   That my
Speech acts
Mustered, I came
   To the practice,
Came with a roomful
A brimful
Then a motion
   Annexed but onscreen
Too much debris
   In their guts

They don't
See it
To compensate
I nod
   To Morosa, Edith,
Isabella, Loreena,
(Sounds like roil)
And they met
   Up to the ones
With tricorns and
   Never-brows
I believe woefully
In reward
   Welcome only
Outlaws who business
With me
His entrée—
   Transported upside
Down by helicopter

The long dark howl
A fool visits
They hear only
    Sprightly containment
And then
Spooling feathers
    Into baskets, that's
The garden-dope
Flush out all
    The live ones
Ear-soft with tomorrow
Blotchy
With peach
Get all mushy
    With the methody
Embrace
Get my procedure?
Violet and zero
    Knowing twat

Largely relaxing
    At the great landed
Estates in their
Orangeries
    And details galore
About their
Habits for the citizens
Truly they sag
But have a metal
    Sheen
I've been a silent
Partner
In the deal, though
Audible
With dream-readings
    A beginner
Reluctantly fastened
    To ire demands

That's product we
Had in mind
    Daisy the pair
Of them
The cloud's a-comin'
Why insist
    It's they
Who drag their
Tongues.
    Go flip it
Heat up the miraculous
I'll be a
Novice
Pronounce it with
    Fur preferring
Deportation then
Wave when the canal
Barge passes

Rollicking soon
Say a one-word
   Command and Oh
That it be
The glossary
Of calls
In an almanac
   All authored up
Then bake
They climatize to it
   I'm remaindered
Speak speak
Clocking around this
   Shady guild
Synonymous with bestow
Shift in order
To change
   Stable in, sincere
As that
   Buy anytime
Off-season
Choose like the race
That it is

When they wrangle
They're talking
   Snowballs, their
Half-baked fisticuffs
   It's the debt that
Hides near
Moss, its iridescence
Gives it
Agency
   Some get drunk
On the orchards
Momentarily ransom
   A harpy eagle
Hold it
Thusly
My medieval fetishes
   I'm practiced
In gawking
Shepherding fills me
   I counsel them
They, me
A shoulder
   Dip a kink in
The tail

Sluggish as dark
   Dye and off-kilter
Heave remotely
Then synchronize
Roars
   Surge near
Decks more chatting
The entire
   Pride blurring
Across the rock face
   Josephine opted
For Empire and
   Enclosures
For the rare
I'm counting
   My efforts in plosives
Spirants
   The coarse rash of
Them guards

Rush ghost-trains
Tell to the three-toed
With scars taut
   And trembling
A red gash—
   That's vermilion to some
She and I watch
Together, hunting
Dogs surround
   From our oasis
There goes
The pepper tree, lacy
And brisk,
   Nimble wing
It's high time
   For southward
Migration
Sincere as you could
Be with
   Outsourcing
With ribbon helixed
In a tree

We nudge
Until the shut down
  View the yard
Sparrow theatrics
All decked
Out in the sky's
  Invisible cells
She and I hung
Up on goodbye,
Dream basket, cottony
  Air—it's middle earth,
Or something
Like that,
Something like
  Calypso
Among alder
And poplar
  With her Polaroid
She snaps
  Spray and showery
Stuff, not
The real bird.

# V

## ARRAIGNMENT

## Inhabited Initial Q

From the curled field and warm corner she may not feel
a bit condemned.

Reverie will run
through it, and she'll flit
right off the topic.

Keepers are puzzled, all that roaring into the light, those hyped-up asterisks.

It's the way a dreamer dreams its double. How still
the last t's are, no vowel to help its pitch.

When wings close in,
scavenge some bloodtipped quills.
Let the misery out,

protect *not* as a mother. In the hollow she wishes a river,
and a ring turns,

one more subtle turn.

You might hear the susurrations
and then a flutter

meant to even the frequency.
Let the nighttime murmur a new pelt.

And they're born, they're born. Padlocked and gruffed, she blunts the circumstance,

repeats her little
work song. Teach dream, teach folly, as though they were manners to acquire.

## ARRAIGNMENT

Wolverine implausibility, wolverine candor,
wolverine turnpike.
I trade my scenery
and wolverine reason,
not an emergency
to disclose.
Wolverine
solution, a school, an annex,
a new job at the factory.

Never called. Wolverine
weight and wolverine ration
from the den.
The date I read
backwards. Wolverine traffic.
Only you can only
think of only
wolverine pause, wolverine
channel.

Warding off fumes. Needs solace
that way. Dug in
and thriving.
Thief of the terrain. Come to the lean-to.
Wolverine triggered.
Wouldn't
answer, wouldn't console.
Moonclaws on white,
wolverine angling, wolverine
tough love.
Notes of shame,
tried in the snow dust.

# THE SOFTENING

When he's shouldering his false idols,

he glances up and closes his eyes. My reflection's in a trough,
a yucca bloom shivers,

explains my blotted out yearning

and the need to be blind and zeroed.
Never did he alarm.
Never did his wits take to the ladders.

I miss the flesh tokens, the way he buried some,
and whether I'll twirl around

and meet his grudges, that remains

to be seen. I'd tweak the dial a bit, shove governing aside,

and lean on his boundaries,
ready to slow

his sway-back,

Ride it out, I urge myself,

and he signals
to his comrades, tusks-ready, jeopardy in place—my pores liven to it.

Shouldn't phantoms keep their distance? Why do they bother
the small ones?

In their haze, they could bend the light.
They could ghost

the terrain and drag the sutured one along.  They nick themselves,
angle in for what's easy.

Some go locking up their wings,

one returns
in his brute way, frets at having gone through the torched sky.

He's kill-exhausted, taped up like a ghetto heap.

So if I honor
his thick hide now, if I take the tasker flying, I might

uncover his junky gray coat, dab his skin with gauze
worn over and over with metal and mesh.

## Dukedoms Are For

sulking, I'd say
to my outcast
friends, and shouldn't
you pay off that witness
and hide out for awhile?
Stars blink on their cheeks
after the fall out.
There's something
about hunger like that,
something dutiful
and deranged that might
zag across the sky's
failures. And I shook off
the refrains I'd carried
for so long, and
let the rainforest usurp
the wide green land.
Now it sounds like
the eons met up with
those shady ones—
they pull their carts
almost careening
from the top-most
branches. What do they
misunderstand? In the end
it's the launch they
longed for.
Oh sweet! The toothless
ones wait by the mailboxes.
looking like governance,
their public side
with its drowse and pageant.

# Tomorrow, Fauna

I guess it's too early to know—
their empty site and unforgiving zone.

There's tugging from the ditches,
I make my plans with chores to bolt from easily. When can I

whisper closely, lean against the pock marks in the fence?

Is that the *somewhere warmer*? Built quietly,

with a bonehouse look.
I'll swear by the fake nighttime to catch up or find neighbors

until they're hunched
into themselves with a muffling hood

of hair. Don't they blink to another face and drag their thickets

along behind?
It doesn't mean much to them when I finally leave.
It never does,

even when I promise a tender brush.
They pass it off and fool with light jokes in their huddles,

and I think they even plan their next disappearance, shed
their buzzing and their fluff.

I could be a turncoat

and lead them
in another way, but you wouldn't want
to starve the onlookers—

you wouldn't want to sink the whole day
like that, without leaving a shred of legend.

# HEIRS

If squinting made them
all sail steady,

I'd try to find them that way. Their oval terrain I'd learn. Who else
wants it?

I've been stung
with a green heart and dragged

out backwards. That one snaps
and a year of ashes appear. Its bouldered head shifts and leans into its breeze.
Hoofprints deface

the little earth. Land of no requirements

and the sadness of not
listening. Sounds are just too wide. Here's one who gallops against the rules.

Aloneness is an image to work with so I sketch it
along the divots in the soil. I tick

gently to the voice-overs.

New members come around
lately, and I invite them
to see the armature. Because

now my knees are tired. Because now the faint reek
settles into musk.

Because now I'm deaf
to where the clock leads me.

Some are browsers
and frolic in an underworld.

The service there is witty. One sneers at the hills
folding against

the flat vista. It huffs
into its own squared chest. I could climb on its back and tour the lawlessness.

# VI

## CURRENTS

current . . . safe . . . haunches


. . . where they're rooted . . . and I wait . . . see a flash of haunches . . .
we settled in . . . swelling against . . . reveal brown currents . . . what's caught . . .

the heat . . . I relieve the worry . . . give them stars, praise . . . their thin hooves
. . . a whiff of burlap . . . a just soft enough gamble . . . .

. . . settled in at the enclosure . . . I'd see how to be rooted . . . the gentle relief

. . . camouflage . . . except for the white breaks . . . housed where the roots and

creek bed meet . . . I've starred their return . . . thin currents . . . a new covering
. . . with a line running beside . . . hind with a crown . . .

hutch . . . trophy . . . hide


. . . there its eyelid . . . strains for the blossom . . . I pressed on up . . .

keep near . . . going for the trophy . . . they hide in a hutch . . . with streams

sounding I wade in . . . narrow enough . . . let them hear . . . some fold . . . .

. . . onto the steep path . . . looking close . . . their hutch hidden . . . sutured up
and wide-eyed . . . they prowl, remember the dispatch . . . steeper . . . .

. . . by the minute . . . I shouldn't . . . my eyelids heavy . . . I whisper close . . .
to yours . . . trophy to what is hidden . . . .

branches . . . tawny . . . dread . . . disappear


I've slowed . . . trying invisibility . . . they pull at the upper most branches
. . . their sleek necks . . . each in turn . . . motor noises slowing . . . and tawny grass

. . . disappear . . . I elegize, dreading it . . . as afternoon tries to slow . . . lie down . . . .

. . . they stomp above the motors . . . through the grasses . . . my ears disappear . . .

sounds are dreaded . . . they sway . . . laboring and slow . . . smaller time
. . . abandoned to . . . slapping the days down . . . dispossessed . . .

and dreadful falling branches . . . soft fur near their temples . . . lean in

slow but disappearing . . . mine too, turned . . . .

heavy . . . mark . . . sorry


. . . I'd take back the threat . . . the heavy . . . and in the dark, huffs . . .

even in moonlight . . . against rough walls . . . how sorry keeps . . .
tracking the absences . . . with thuds, barks . . . retreats . . . they, the villains

talk without tongues . . . black markings . . . sorry behind me . . . now ahead . . . .

. . . rough little grottoes . . . how they show with thuds . . . their heavy tracks

. . . knew what's better for them . . . I was . . . they're absent now . . .
I plumb the grottoes and heavy walls . . . the sorry show of moonlight . . .

on route they thud . . . they show themselves . . . .

tunnel . . . leaves . . . empty

What's mattering with it . . . spray blossom . . . full load . . . sullen petals . . .

dark allergens . . . fuel the downtown escape . . . more meddling . . .
I knelt to the mud . . . better than dried up leaves . . . pillowy leads to tunnels . . . .

. . . solace on the turnpike . . . fake it or buzz naturally . . . I'd be harboring . . .

mutters . . . like its natural self . . . petals around its brow . . . back up nurse

. . . the more I felt its limbo . . . looming cedars, stay-aloft oaks . . . leaves stammer

underneath . . . which one of them . . . held steady . . . in spite of the bidding . . . .

# Library

*The Animal Side,* Jean-Christophe Bailly, (trans. Catherine Porter), Fordham University Press, 2011.

*Why Look at Animals?* John Berger, Penguin Books, 1980.

*Clara's Grand Tour: Travels with a Rhinocerous in Eighteenth-Century Europe,* Glynis Ridley, Grove Press, 2004.

*History of Earth and Animated Nature,* Oliver Goldsmith, 1807.

The Los Angeles Zoo and Botanical Gardens

## Acknowledgements

Thank you to the editors of the following journals in which some of the poems first appeared, sometimes in different versions:

*Apercus Quarterly, Black Tongue Review, Cincinnati Review, Colorado Review, Denver Quarterly, Drunken Boat, Fairy Tale Review, Lana Turner: Journal of Poetry and Opinion, New American Writing, Omniverse, Specs, The Offending Adam, Verse, Volt, Yew Journal.*

My deepest gratitude and love to Daniel Tiffany and many thanks also to Cal Bedient, Jon Thompson, John O'Brien, Vidhu Aggarwal, Gail Wronsky, Rodney Jones, Judith Taylor, Brenda Hillman, and Rusty Morrison.

And thank you to everyone at Omnidawn.